LIGHT YOUR CHURCH ON FIRE WITHOUT BURNING IT DOWN

CHURCH IN THE 21ST CENTURY
Volume One

DAVID HOUSHOLDER
Hunting

D1044525

Copyright © 2009 David Housholder
All rights reserved.

ISBN: 1-4392-3731-X
ISBN-13: 9781439237311
LCCN: 2009903630

Contact the author: ThornHeart.com
Listen to his iTunes podcast: RobinwoodChurch.com

Visit www.booksurge.com to order additional copies.

"I have personally sat under David Housholder's teaching on this topic, and I invite you to read this book and open yourself up to the potent, awareness-changing presence of the Holy Spirit in your life."

Ken Blanchard
Author of *The One Minute Manager*

✧ ✧ ✧

"Christianity without an active and ongoing relationship with the person and work of the Holy Spirit will not work. God designed the church to be in conversation with the Holy Spirit. Yet we all know that can be a scary proposition. We need reliable guides to help us get there. Dave Housholder and his book *Light Your Church on Fire Without Burning it Down* are just such guides. You'll find a way to all the right stuff while navigating around the rough waters of the weirdness you may fear."

Todd Hunter
Pastor: Holy Trinity Anglican Church, Costa Mesa, CA
Director: Churches for the Sake of Others, The Anglican Mission

✧ ✧ ✧

"David Housholder has prepared this delightful cross-cultural guide book for curious Christians to explore the marvelous world of Pentecostals and Charismatics. If you don't completely understand the Pentecostal religious experience, and if you don't know the exact vocabulary surrounding the Spirit-filled life, this book is for you! Housholder translates his own spiritual journey with vivid definitions and insightful images. He describes his experience with the baptism of the Spirit as akin to getting a spiritual tattoo. This book's goal is to allow the reader to see afresh, deeply appreciate, and fall in love - again - with the Holy Spirit."

The Rev. Dr. Richard Bliese
President, Luther Seminary
St. Paul, Minnesota

✡ ✡ ✡

"This is a blast—fun to read, intellectually satisfying and leading straight to experiential faith. David Housholder is uniquely positioned to produce this book. His very formal education coupled with a wide-open personality set him up to mine the depths of the powerful work of the Spirit bursting upon the 21st Century. A must read for anyone wanting to go deeper with God!"

Ralph Moore
Founder of the Hope Chapels
Author of *How To Multiply Your Church*

✡ ✡ ✡

DEDICATED TO:

Wendy, my ever-patient bride

Paul Anderson, who encouraged me to be myself,
for the first time, spiritually

CONTENTS:

Did you receive the Holy Spirit when you believed?
— Paul

We have not even heard that there is a Holy Spirit…
— The Ephesians

ACKNOWLEDGEMENTS

This is the part you wish was not so long when you watch the Academy Awards.

First of all, I'd like to thank dear colleague and missional pastor Bob Rognlien (ExperientialWorship.com) for pestering me for months to write this book. Thanks also to Eric, Dana, and Steve from the group that meets twice a year to encourage each other's writing.

Thanks also to Ann Louise Huffman, who has no idea I am writing this book. Her prayer (see Chapter One below) over another man in a healing service scared me into a whole new world—the world of the supernatural.

Thanks to J.E. Danielson, Marinus Vermeer, Thomas Housholder, and to the Rev. Maynard Nelson, who are now all with the Lord but were among my main vocational "shapers." I still want to be just like them when I grow up.

Thanks to the Rev. Bill Bohline of Hosanna! in Lakeville, Minnesota (HosannaLC.org), who gave me and others unbelievable freedom in putting into practice all that we were learning about the Holy Spirit.

Thanks to Nicky Gumbel and all my dear colleagues who teach the Alpha Course (alpha.org), which has given me a worldwide outlet for telling of my experiences with the living God.

Thanks to the saints at Robinwood Church (RobinwoodChurch.com) in Huntington Beach, California, which is the purest expression of a Spirit-filled congregation I have ever seen.

And thanks to Ken Blanchard (*The One Minute Manager*), who suggested I publish this on BookSurge.

Huntington Beach, California
Summer 2009

Chapter One
THE PROBLEM

If you picked up this book, you most likely identify
yourself as a Christian, or at least by your denominational
title (Evangelical, Lutheran, Methodist, Roman Catholic,
etc.). Perhaps you even like going to church. There is a
good chance that you are quite active in your congregation
and committed to the cause of Christ.

But I'm convinced that you are fascinated and maybe
even troubled by the topic of the Holy Spirit.

If your church uses creeds, you recite, maybe even weekly,
that you "believe in the Holy Spirit."

But what does that mean?

You may have run into Christians who have a certain
temperamental abandon, a "zeal," if you will, about the
Holy Spirit. There may even be a little group of them
in your established church who identify themselves

as "Charismatics." You may be attracted to them and unnerved by them at the same time.

When it comes down to it, you may feel left out of a party that you're not sure you want to attend!

In most churches like yours, very few people are fluent in talking about the Holy Spirit. They may not even know what pronouns to use. Your minister may even refer to the Holy Spirit as "it" in sermons on Pentecost Sunday (the liturgical celebration of the coming of the Spirit and the birthday of the Christian Church).

Well, you've bought the right book.

The truth is however, you are probably not putting this book in plain sight for others to see. You have stepped out of your comfort zone by reading this page.

I am going to introduce you to the person and work of the Holy Spirit, and the whole world of Charismatic and Pentecostal Christianity.

The two groups (Charismatic and Pentecostal) overlap a lot.

The modern Pentecostal movement started in 1906 at Azusa Street in Los Angeles, California. What began in an underprivileged multiracial congregation has become the fastest growing religious movement in human history. If trends continue, Pentecostal Christians could outnumber not only Roman Catholics but also Muslims in your lifetime.

"Charismatic" is a label for Pentecostal Christians within non-Pentecostal denominations. Charismatics tend to have the same flavor as Pentecostals, but are a bit more toned-down (they have to get along with their neighbors) and understated. There are Charismatics in all of the "mainline" Protestant denominations and a staggeringly huge number of them who would also identify themselves as Roman Catholics.

I will often refer to them both under one or the other heading during the course of this book. Unless you're really picky, the terms can be seen as interchangeable in casual conversation.

I'd like to be clear, from the very start, that I don't speak for all Charismatics and Pentecostals. Some of them may disagree with some of my conclusions. The views in this book are purely my own. However, I am speaking from *inside* the movement and I understand Pentecostal motivations and behavior patterns fairly well. My views are common and typical within the main currents of the movement.

What makes Pentecostals tick is that they are highly *experience-oriented* and emphasize the supernatural over the theological. The narration (theology, storytelling, etc.) surrounding their movement, although important, is secondary to the actual encounter with God.

Many outsiders feel profoundly uncomfortable in their meetings. The energy level is high, and it feels as if almost anything could happen. A high percentage of their congregations are small, and the pastors may seem, to outsiders, to lack theological training. Most of these pastors have other jobs during the week.

On the other hand, chances are, if you are a part of a name-brand church, you have Charismatic members in your midst. They follow your congregation's patterns and customs, but have a different "tone" about them. You may hear them mumble little things during group prayer. One or two of them may discreetly have raised their hands during the singing of "How Great Thou Art."

You may also have encountered full-blown Pentecostal worship (on their "home field" in one of their own churches) if you are the type that gets out a lot and is uninhibited.

When regular church members encounter Pentecostals, they often feel inadequate to have a conversation. They don't even know the vocabulary, and they certainly don't share the experiential base. Many such self-designated "Spirit-filled" types also come across as prideful or as "having something that you don't have." They are often unaware of this and truly aren't trying to be arrogant. But this doesn't help things.

They even give testimonies in their meetings about how they used to be like you and other conventional Christians, but now they "get it." Listening to such talk can be offensive to those of us raised in historical, established churches.

The purpose of this book is to overcome this "distance" many may feel between themselves and Pentecostal-Charismatic Christians. Think of me as a cross-cultural tour guide.

I am, personally speaking, totally bi-lingual. I was raised deep in traditional Lutheranism. There are four ordained Lutheran pastors in my family. Two of my great-grandfathers were "klokkers" in Norwegian Hauge Synod Lutheran churches (the klokkers were the ones who rang the church bell, led songs, and led prayer meetings).

I am also very comfortable in the hottest of Pentecostal prayer meetings and am very much a part of their culture. I am, everywhere in the world that I go, accepted among them as one of their insiders.

What historical accident provided for this?

I was a Lutheran church planter on the Olympic Peninsula of Washington State. Classically educated, I had just finished Fulbright Scholarship work in Germany. I was somewhat of an expert in liturgy and knew my way around Lutheran systematic theology.

In the gullies and gulches of the Olympic Peninsula, visiting people to try to build up my new little church, I ran into a different kind of Christian.

I was totally unprepared for what I found and for what it was going to do to me.

These people spoke in tongues, laid on hands for healing, would occasionally shout and dance, and talked about God with a sparkle in their eyes that I had never seen before.

To make a long story short, I ended up becoming one of them, without giving up on who I had been. I did not have a "conversion," I just took on a second citizenship. I didn't stop being Lutheran. I didn't stop being an educated theologian. But at some point, I did become Pentecostal.

I was immediately drawn to them like a moth to flame. First of all, they had a ton of entertainment value. There was a lot of drama that had been lacking in my controlled Euro-Christianity. Second of all, they seemed to get "at" a primary form of Christianity for which I only had secondary reflections.

They knew Jesus in a way that I wanted to know him.

I remember being at a healing meeting with them after church (I had long since invited them to join our new little congregation). One of the women started singing over someone in tongues. I leaned in to listen and was totally unprepared for what was about to happen. Jolting through my mind were the exact English words for what she was singing. Not some "feeling" about an interpretation's sense—the actual words, in English. And I couldn't get them out of my head.

I left the meeting, immediately, in a panic. I don't even smoke, but wanted a cigarette—badly. Pacing in my office down the hall, I asked God, "What was *that*?" I asked it out loud. I may have even used a bad word or two, which would be impolite to print in this book.

Of course, I had just received the gift of *interpretation of tongues*. I had never even spoken in tongues, let alone interpreted. It was, capriciously and randomly, given by God—and I had not asked for it. I still operate in the gift, and it's something I've never "learned."

While "leaning in" to the healing prayer, my defenses, my shields, were down. And, in rushed the Holy Spirit.

My breathing changes and my skin tingles to this day, every time I think of the experience at that healing meeting.

That was lesson one. There were many lessons to come.

These Pentecostal believers gave me an experiential base to match my theological training and teaching. It all fit together perfectly. The whole book of Galatians and the eighth chapter of Romans took on meaning that had previously escaped me.

In a way, I got spiritual "tattoos" among them. They are impossible to scrub off.

I can't imagine a person who has experienced these things ever becoming "ex-Pentecostal." The spiritual ink is way too indelible.

What I would like to do, in this book, is to share what I have learned, and what I have become.

It will help you understand us.

Chapter Two
FLUENCY IN CONVERSATION ABOUT THE HOLY SPIRIT

Not a lot of Christians are used to talking about the Holy Spirit in a casual and personal way.

Members of mainstream churches may face language problems every time they try to talk to Pentecostals.

They, and perhaps you, aren't highly practiced in how to talk about the Holy Spirit.

We, *outside* of Pentecostal circles, have been heavily influenced, in our Holy Spirit grammar, by the New Age movement and by feminism.

New Agers, who use the term "Holy Spirit" (or just "Spirit" without a pronoun) a lot (e.g., many *Course in Miracles* folks), tend to use the pronoun "it" for the Holy Spirit.

Activists for "inclusive language" in mainline churches do back-flips to avoid saying "he" for the Holy Spirit. Most of this well-meant usage is informed by Christian feminism. (Not that I have anything against gender egalitarianism in its Christian or secular forms. I and many Pentecostals and Charismatics lean "egalitarian" in our temperament and practice.)

The line of reasoning that follows is not meant to be strident or political. It is meant to aid communication. Please receive it in the helpful spirit in which it is intended.

This above-mentioned pronoun deficit and lack of clarity leaves most mainline Christians at a distinct disadvantage when talking about Holy Spirit experiences. They get tangled, quickly, in grammar problems, insecurities, and lack of "non-self-conscious language."

If you've ever tried to speak a second language in a foreign country (i.e., trying to use your high school Spanish in Mexico), you know what I mean.

First of all, I just want to say that you can call the Holy Spirit anything you want. You can use him, her, or it—any name you choose. I am not here to control your language.

But if you want to communicate with the ones who talk about the Holy Spirit the most, you will need a vocabulary. And the Pentecostals control, worldwide, over 95% of the direct discourse about the Holy Spirit. At least!

First of all, if you ever use the pronoun "it" for the Holy Spirit, you may well be written off by Pentecostals or Charismatics as someone who doesn't see the Spirit as personal, but rather as an impersonal "force." You will not, in such circles, get respect for yourself talking like this. In football terms, they will assume you don't know the playbook.

The point of communication is communication. If you insist on idiosyncratic language usage, you will be sidelined by those who control the conversation. And there are hundreds of millions of them, and only a few of you.

I surf most days at the pier in Huntington Beach, California, a few blocks from my home. Some of the best surfers in America control the lineup there. If I want to get a wave, I have to fit in with those who know the wave the best. The Pentecostals control the "Holy Spirit talk" wave; we need to fit in.

If you use "she/her" for the Holy Spirit (and there are good reasons for doing so, both in the Hebrew and the Greek), you will also get written off by the Pentecostals. You certainly will not be able to participate fully in their activities saying "she" for the Spirit.

If you go to Spain, use Spanish. If you hang out with Pentecostals, use Pentecostal language.

For them, the Holy Spirit is "he/him."

There really are no exceptions. They had to choose a *personal* pronoun, so "it" was out from the beginning.

And the twin pillars of the English language, German and Latin, both use a masculine pronoun, endings, articles, and declensions for *Geist* and *Spiritus.* In fact, these two nouns themselves are incurably masculine. All you have to do is listen to our poetry and hymnody to see and "get" this.

Thus, to try and make Holy Ghost or Holy Spirit feminine among Pentecostals is pushing water uphill. Good luck.

I run in lots of Pentecostal circles and have never heard the masculinity of the Holy Spirit emphasized, other than linguistically. The Holy Spirit is beyond gender, but not ever impersonal. This usage is simply common labeling, which works for them. And it's not going to change.

Ironically, it can be patronizing and imperialistic to impose your/our pronoun use on a (huge) subculture that is doing fine without our help.

As my mom says, when you visit people, be a good guest.

In a nutshell, the Holy Spirit/Ghost, in the Pentecostal world, takes a masculine personal pronoun, but has no other masculine attributes or even implications. Pentecostals ordained women into full pastoral leadership *long* before liberal Protestants even thought of it. Some Pentecostal denominations (e.g., The Foursquare Church) were even founded by women.

If you were to say, for instance, "When the Holy Spirit came upon us, it [or she] was all over the place," you will get a lot of "You're not from around here, are you?" looks.

If you want to talk with them, those are the rules. We don't get to write the rules. They already have.

Before moving on to chapter three, I want to make a huge clarification.

Pentecostals get very upset that liberal, mainline, and Roman Catholic Christians continue to lump them in with Baptists and other non-Pentecostal conservative evangelical Christians.

Very, very few Baptists are Charismatic or Pentecostal. Many of their congregations define themselves as folks who don't do the things Pentecostals do. Many Baptists who admit they speak in tongues end up getting the "left foot of fellowship." In fact, recently, the Southern Baptist Convention came down hard on their foreign missionaries who operate in this gift.

Conservative Christians who are anti-Pentecostal (the extreme reaches of conservative Christianity) can be called "cessationists."

Cessationists (a form of dispensationalism, the topic of a whole 'nother book) teach that the more clearly supernatural spiritual gifts ceased when the last apostle died. They believe that tongues and healing (especially those two gifts) are not for today. God just used them to get the church started. Now that we have the canon (accepted books) of the New Testament, we no longer need them.

Don't assume that all non-Roman Catholic or non-liberal or non-mainline Protestants are all the same.

In fact, Pentecostal congregations, along with being forerunners in the ordination of women, are, to this day, some of the only racially integrated churches you can find anywhere.

Most Pentecostals assume a conservative Evangelical theology, but their emphasis, as we shall continue to state, is on the *encounter* with God and not on the explanation.

Evangelicals come in at least two major flavors:

1) Pentecostal/Charismatic
2) Non-Charismatic Conservative Evangelical (most Baptists and "Bible Churches")

Not noticing and appreciating the difference is like confusing the Japanese for Chinese, or vice versa. It won't go well.

You will travel better in these circles if you are familiar with this crucial distinction.

Chapter Three
WHO, OR WHAT, IS THE HOLY SPIRIT?

For many of us who grew up in historical congregations, the Holy Spirit lived somewhere in the Apostles' Creed and he didn't get out much.

I can honestly say, and I was in church almost every Sunday for my entire childhood, that I never heard anyone talk personally about the Holy Spirit.

I grew up in a silver- and lead-mining town where people used *really* foul language—a lot. I had a Ph.D. in profanity by the time I was ten. But the Holy Spirit even got left out of the cuss words!

In much of systematic theology, the Holy Spirit is relegated to "sanctification" or the holy-making of people. Justification and salvation are reserved for Jesus, the Son. Creation is reserved for the Father.

But if you look at the conversion stories in the book of Acts, the Holy Spirit gets more ink than Jesus does.

The most common term for conversion in the
New Testament is "Spirit filling."

In fact, Paul was so "Pentecostal" (granted, this is a
retrofitted term) that he would scare most contemporary
Pentecostals.

The truth is, most conservative non-Pentecostal
Protestant theologians love Paul's theology, but his
spirituality scares the bejeebers out of them. The same
could be said for mainline Protestant theologians and
how they view Paul.

You see, Paul's conversion was a spiritual event, an
encounter. It was not just saying "yes" to any teaching
or message. It was not based on repentance alone. He
just got hammered by the living Christ on the road
to Damascus. Paul's theology, his explanation of what
happened to him, was, thus, heavily encounter-based.

And this is the experience that Paul offered people, from
town to town. He did not peddle a disembodied teaching
with no supernatural content.

He laid hands on people, and the Holy Spirit came. Upon Jew
and Gentile. Upon men and women. Upon slave and free.

The Holy Spirit came, and he rewired their entire inner
beings. Communities were created around this experience
of grace and power.

For Paul, salvation was not primarily a cognitive event. It wasn't just saying "yes" to a particular teaching or doctrine. It was a powerful encounter with the living God that left smoke coming out of the ears of the recipients.

For Paul, the nature of this God had a lot of internal overlap. He lacked the legal description of the Holy Spirit to which those in later centuries would come.

Paul did not have the Trinity all figured out. That came later in history. For him, the Spirit of Jesus and the Holy Spirit were more or less the same person.

For Paul, in a nutshell, the Holy Spirit can only be found deep inside of us. We can't find him in the externals (law, rules, etc.), and we can't find him with our senses. The irony is, that although he is to be found in our inner world, his origin is from far beyond us (transcendent). He is not contained by our personhood. He is within us but from somewhere else, and he doesn't depend on us for his being.

Jesus is the easiest person of the Trinity to figure out (although his divine/human nature has caused theological fights for centuries). He is our gateway to the Father and to the Spirit. God is called Father with increased frequency when Jesus starts talking about him as such. I became a father when my son was born. Of course, any analogy between God and me breaks down pretty quickly, but you get the point.

Jesus also sends us and shows us the Spirit. The Bible tells us that Jesus is the "baptizer in the Holy Spirit."

Thus Jesus is, for us, the central person of the Trinity. After all, we are called Christians, not "Fatherians" or "Spiritists." Jesus shows us all of God.

It helps to continue to see, in this sense, the Holy Spirit as the Spirit of Jesus, just like Paul did. For Paul, Jesus showed up with the Holy Spirit.

And this Holy Spirit is better known by experiencing him than by learning about him from teachers or books.

My fondest wish is that you will set this book aside and yield to his presence.

I can just guide you to the seashore. It will be up to you to immerse yourself in the water.

And immerse yourself you will.

The water is way deeper than you can imagine.

Chapter Four
WHAT IS "SPIRIT FILLING"?

Pentecostals often ask each other, "Is she/he Spirit filled?"

There may be no phrase, in these circles, that is more common.

It is a form of code language that defines who's in and who's out.

Before you get upset about this, every group on earth, by its very definition, has the right to decide who is in and who is out. I am not a Muslim, I am not French, and no statements by me to the contrary will make any difference. The Muslims and the French get to decide who is Muslim and who is French.

Pentecostalism is the fellowship of the Spirit filled.

According to *their* definition, by the way.

If you insist that all the water-baptized are automatically and fully Spirit filled, the conversation with Pentecostals will end. And you will bear the burden of proof, since the Bible clearly states that there is a contrast between water baptism and Spirit/fire baptism.

The conversion stories in the book of Acts pivot around this phrase ("Spirit filling") and the experience it describes.

Most typical historical-church attendees don't know how to interpret the question "Is she/he Spirit filled?" much less answer it.

It isn't a part of their normal parlance.

Pentecostalism (and arguably, the earliest church) is experience-based, not theology-based. And that central experience is called being "filled with the Spirit."

There is such a thing as Pentecostal theology. Some of it is actually, for a young movement, quite sophisticated. However, this body of teaching is primarily *descriptive* of things God does to us and of our experiences of these very real things.

Pentecostal theology is, thus, not speculative in nature. It grows out of an encounter. And their primary "apologetic" is to lay hands on you and ask the Spirit to come upon you, not to argue you into the faith by reasoning.

Pentecostals would rather experience the grace of God than to teach on it.

Before going any further, I want to talk about the important distinction Pentecostals make between being *indwelt* by the Holy Spirit and being *filled* with the Holy Spirit.

All Christian believers are indwelt by the Holy Spirit. They could not have come to faith without the presence of the Holy Spirit within them.

But not all believers are filled with the Holy Spirit. In fact, many Pentecostals will say that there are times and seasons when they, themselves, are not filled with the Spirit.

All believers have a pilot light of the Holy Spirit, but not all of us have turned the full flame up all the time. We go through empty periods when God seems distant.

In fact the "unforgivable sin against the Holy Spirit" can be described as blowing out the pilot light. That would be bad. Not a perfect analogy, but it works at a certain level.

So how do we get filled with the Spirit?

We cannot achieve the experience. We cannot "work it up."

We cannot meditate or "yoga-ize" our way in.

We certainly cannot get there by good works.

There is one word and one word alone that describes how to get filled with the Spirit.

And that word is: yielding.

We have to give up all decorum, all respectability, and all social control. We have to let it happen. We have to let 'er rip.

Many Anglo North Americans and Western Europeans have a really hard time with this. They are a deeply self-conscious lot. "Letting go" is almost impossible for many of them to do, especially around other people. And *super*-especially in church.

Someone equated being filled with the Spirit as standing on your toes, backwards, on a high-dive diving platform (like the way-up-there ones in the Olympics), and then letting yourself fall backwards through the air and into the deep water.

And not trying to catch yourself, brace yourself, or move in any way. To become one with the act of "falling."

It is the ultimate act of risking and trusting.

To be filled with the Spirit, you have to give up any concern for the expectations of those around you. Or what you might tell people tomorrow about the experience. You can't control the experience or the story about it.

You have to be willing to lose yourself in God.

All human beings are just seconds away from the experience. We just have to let go and let it happen.

Sounds may come out of your mouth that you don't understand. Deep solutions and insights may suddenly occur to you. You may find your hands rising above your head without you putting them there. You may start to dance without choosing your steps. You may collapse and fall over. You breathing may become odd; tears may well and splash. You may feel warm, or even hot. You may pass out and enter a trance (yes, "trance" is a biblical term).

But the main thing you will feel is the love and grace of God. Have a look at Ephesians 3:14 and following. This is what Paul is describing.

It is a deep inner journey, but the irony is (we've mentioned this before) that the experience does not come from inside of us, but rather from beyond us.

The past disappears, as does the future. All that remains is the present. And God.

You can call this "person" you encounter the risen Christ, the Father and his love, the Holy Spirit, the Word/Logos, the Spirit of Christ, or even the Shekinah Glory (said with a shouting Southern accent), and you will be right. We believe in one biblical God: the God of Abraham, Isaac, and Jacob.

When you get filled with the Holy Spirit, you experience all of the living God at once, even though one label may be the most useful for you. Specific labels and/or attributes are less important. They are secondary.

Remember, theology is secondary to encounter. God does not depend on his definitions.

The important thing, and the only thing, is that you and God show up in the present, together. Here and now.

Fear of death vanishes, as does guilt for sin. As does stress about our worldly surroundings.

We experience salvation. A true Pentecostal would say, "What's the use of having salvation if you don't experience it? If you don't feel grace, how can you know it?"

This "Spirit filling" overlaps, perhaps entirely, with the concept of being "baptized in the Spirit." Both are solid biblical phrases that cannot be explained away. The Bible even draws a contrast (mentioned earlier) between being baptized with water and being baptized with the Spirit.

Thus, the Bible does not teach that they are identical. In fact, if push comes to shove, it is impossible to prove that the baptism commands in the New Testament are even about water at all, including the Great Commission at the end of Matthew. The Quakers continue to remind us of this, and they happen to be right.

Spirit filling can happen during music, when outdoors in the beauty of nature, or during prayer ministry.

Prayer ministry, or as Charismatics and Pentecostals call it, "ministry time," usually happens in the last major segment of a meeting or church service. It is a big part of the "liturgy" or Pentecostal worship. It is, in a way, a sacrament.

You could argue that many Pentecostals (although they don't explicitly systematize or rank it), in practice if not in theory, have several sacraments, in order of importance:

1) Prayer ministry (including healing prayer, Spirit filling, etc.)
2) Worship and praise
3) Water baptism
4) Holy communion

By the way, many Pentecostals and Charismatics expect people to come to faith during communion (i.e., conversion), and thus often don't limit it to believers. And water baptism, for them, although important, is secondary to Spirit baptism/filling.

Back to prayer ministry...

People come forward to trained prayer ministers for prayer. They open up their hands in front of them, and the prayer ministers lay hands on the person's shoulders or head.

And God is invited in.

The purpose of prayer ministry is to connect the needs of the person with the power of God. The prayer ministers themselves will be the first to say that they do not work miracles. They are just conduits.

The first time you go forward for prayer ministry (if you have not already) can be a profoundly moving experience. I remember the first time I went forward in Arizona. I could hardly breathe.

Spirit filling, in Pentecostal circles, most often happens in the context of ministry time. The classic question is asked: "How can I pray for you?" You could answer: "I would like to pray to be filled with the Holy Spirit."

Different Pentecostal and Charismatic groups will put different amounts of emphasis on speaking in tongues and its connection to Spirit filling. There will be more on this later.

For now, you just need to know that classical Pentecostal groups will be very likely to expect you to speak in tongues as evidence you are truly being filled with the Spirit. This viewpoint, central a century ago, is becoming more and more a minority opinion within the movement.

The problem is, that focusing on these expectations (i.e., the ability to speak in tongues) can actually *hinder* the experience. Then whole idea of Spirit filling is letting go of all expectations (including tongues) and focusing on God alone.

So, let's say that you have asked for prayer to be filled with the Holy Spirit. The prayer ministers will simply ask the Spirit to come. According to the Gospel of Luke, God's answer to this prayer is always "yes."

Once again, don't let your focus wander off of God. And the Holy Spirit will come.

Very occasionally, the results will be disappointing. There can be a number of causes for this:

1) The prayer ministers were distracting to you, and they took your focus off of God.
2) You have areas of control in your life you are not willing to give up.
3) You struggle with great self-consciousness.
4) You have been abused and have erected many defenses, which guard your heart. God bless you for surviving your abuse. Please get help and healing. It can be found.

5) You are striving for the experience rather than yielding to it.
6) Fear that God will *not* show up.
7) A sense of your unworthiness.
8) Fear that God *will* show up! ☺
9) Pride (i.e., "I don't need this.")
10) Something else not on the list!

The problem is not on God's end. He wants to encounter you 24/7. God has more talk than you have listen and is not playing some kind of cosmic shell game with you. God does not play hide-and-seek with us. In the Garden of Eden, *we* were the ones hiding in the bushes. We still are.

If you are having trouble experiencing God's power and grace, try to figure out which of these ten things is "keeping this from happening."

But you don't actually need anyone around, prayer ministers or others, to get filled with the Spirit.

You can set this book aside, open your hands up, and let yourself, spiritually speaking, fall off of the back of the diving platform.

Others can help, but you only need God to dance the dance.

Chapter Five
SPEAKING IN TONGUES

This topic has done more to divide Pentecostal Christians from historical Christians than any other.

To outsiders, speaking in tongues may seem wild, strange, or even creepy.

Many have written off Pentecostalism, because they simply want to have nothing to do with speaking in tongues.

And who could blame them?

Who would put "speaks in tongues" on a résumé? Who would share this ability on a first date? Who would paste it up on Facebook? Who would burst out in tongues during "saying grace" at a big family Thanksgiving dinner?

Although exotic, it also seems strange, and not always strange "in a good way."

Historical seminaries and divinity schools do not have classes in it, and it doesn't happen at their chapel services.

You can be a Christian your whole life and never have heard anyone speak in tongues.

But listen, very, very closely, in almost any church, when the energy gets rolling during a rousing song or praise chorus. You will hear singing that is not following the rest of the group. Listen more closely, and you will notice that it is not using grammar or vocabulary either. This "singing in the Spirit" is actually singing in tongues, and many people don't even know they are doing it.

I would like to de-mythologize speaking in tongues for you. I would like to explain it so that it is less odd and certainly less offensive. In truth, it is beautiful—even, at times, sublime.

Let's start with the study of linguistics (oddly enough, the word means "tongue stuff"). Speaking in tongues, linguistically, is called "glossolalia." It means "expressing oneself vocally without the structures of grammar and/or vocabulary."

It is the mother tongue of us all. Each of us is born using glossolalia exclusively. Only later is a grid of grammar and vocabulary imposed upon our words. We call this "learning to speak." In fact, we have been speaking all along.

There is a certain purity to speech that is not pre-shaped. Think of the squealing of junior high girls running down a hallway, or the battle cry of a football team; the wailing at a funeral, or the belly-laughter that you can't control.

Speaking/singing/praying in tongues is nothing more and nothing less than using this primal language, which we all have, to communicate with God.

Paul talks about this in Romans 8:26ff when he says that the Spirit intercedes for us in groans that cannot be expressed in words.

The Pentecostal movement has simply recovered this form of primal speech for use in prayer and praise.

But doesn't speaking in tongues have to be interpreted? Didn't Paul put strict guidelines on tongues?

Yes and no.

If you are praying to God, using the "passing gear" of glossolalia, then:

1) God does not need an interpreter.
2) As Romans 8:26–27 says, it includes "groans which cannot be expressed in words." If you could have prayed it in English, you would have. The whole idea of using tongues is when the

grammar and vocabulary of English fail us or
are inadequate. When the Bible says "cannot be
expressed in words," it means "cannot."

The truth is, there is no systematic theology of tongues
usage in the New Testament. Paul only obliquely deals
with the topic. It is hard to know what Paul taught on
tongues since we only have the "disciplinarian Paul"
going after the Corinthians' abuse of this ability.

He also goes after Holy Communion abuse in the same
letter (much more severely than he goes after tongues),
and no one would dream of banning communion, or even
marginalizing it.

It is interesting that those who most would like to see
the gift of tongues disappear are the ones who want to
impose all the rules about its use.

If you take the prohibitions and controls Paul puts on
tongues super-literally, then no one will ever be allowed
to use the gift. For that matter, his controls on Holy
Communion have resulted in some churches having
virtually no one taking communion.

Below is the version of the "command to interpret
tongues" that works for me. Like a pair of shoes, try it on.
If it does or doesn't work for you, that's fine.

Sometimes the Lord sends a word to the community, and the one who "receives" it receives it in tongues. Some people have the gift of reception and listening; others have the gift of explaining and teaching. These are two fundamentally different personal qualities. Sometimes the Lord needs both people to get a message across:

1) One to receive the pure spiritual nature of the message (in pre-English, or tongues).
2) One to make sense of this message for the community.

If this doesn't work for you, that's fine. It just helps me know when to apply the "interpretation command."

It seems counterintuitive to apply this interpretation command to communication directed at (i.e., toward) God. He doesn't need our help or interpretation. He just wants to hear the cry of our hearts.

In a nutshell, in my opinion, speaking in tongues directed *at* God does not have to be interpreted, but a message *from* God to the community in tongues does have to be interpreted for the community. It's the only way I know to make sense of the issue.

In order to speak in tongues, however, you have to be willing to set aside the whole English (or whatever structured language) grid and let your feelings get voiced directly into sounds.

It will appear foolish and beautiful at the same time.

Singing in tongues is also something that can come easily if you yield to it. Next time the music is cranking up in your church, just take an "exit ramp" and start singing what is on your spirit. Let go of grammar and vocabulary and sing out your deepest desires and hurts to the Lord. Let your song interact with the song the rest of the group is singing.

Do whatever you can, at some point in your life, to attend a church where the participants love singing in tongues, where the whole congregation takes this "exit ramp." This "singing in the Spirit" may be one of the most other-worldly experiences a person can have on this planet. Waves of "primal speech" wash over the congregation in swell after swell. Just lose yourself in it.

All of the rest of the "composed" music we listen to is just a derivative form of this primal in-the-moment song.

You know, somewhere deep inside, how the song goes. Some struggle with it. Some have the courage to sing it.

Chapter Six
HEALING

The word "healing" has inbred linguistic roots with the term "salvation."

In German, "Heil" means both healing and salvation. Which is why "Heil Hitler!" was such a scary greeting (i.e., "Salvation Hitler!").

Healing and salvation are not exactly the same things, but the overlap between them, linguistically speaking, is huge.

Pentecostal Christians have an incurable preoccupation with healing. Along with Spirit filling and speaking in tongues, healing takes its central place in the Pentecostal "trinity."

American popular media has shied away from tongues and Spirit filling (a little too potent for TV), but they are attracted to Pentecostals, with great fascination, when it comes to healing.

The charlatan healer has become a staple archetype in American film and TV. Most young people can do a passable impersonation of such a character for their friends, for comic relief: "Jesus" (said in five syllables) "heals" (two syllables) in a thick Southern accent.

But it is hard to imagine Pentecostal Christianity without a heavy healing component.

The twentieth century has seen great medical triumphs (polio, smallpox, bypass operations, etc.) and also total medical impotence (AIDS, cancer, or even the common cold).

What a stage for the Pentecostal healer to stride out upon.

There is a strident insistence among Pentecostals that Jesus *meant business* when he was healing, that he intended to send us out to do it (i.e., heal others), and that our abilities in this area far outstrip our faith.

These folks also provide a powerful corrective to the modern Western medical establishment. They continue to insist that healing is primarily *ministry to the core of the person*, not to the symptoms and externals.

Pentecostal healing is deeply non-materialistic.

It is a belief that there are three realms. Romans 8, perhaps the most sublime chapter in the entire Bible, lays this out in profound sophistication.

The first floor in the human being is the "flesh." It includes both our sinful nature and our "temple." We are to be a temple for the Spirit. The body is thus good and bad. It is a paradoxical part of our being.

The second floor, the command center, is the "self." It encompasses the mind, soul, will, emotions, mind, heart, and ego. It is that part of you that is in the driver's seat. It is the "bridge" of your aircraft carrier. It is the part of you that chose to read this.

The third floor is your spirit—your truest self—but not your most conscious or reflective self (that would be the second floor). This is the part that connects with God, because God is "spirit."

Aristotle believed that the first floor was primary. It's what we can observe. So, also, believes modern positivistic science and modern medicine.

Plato believed in the primacy of the second floor, the realm of ideas (remember the "cave" from *The Republic*?) Thus, platonic love is pure love divested of physical/flesh lust. Rationalists and idealists of all kinds have put the center of their gravity on floor two.

Jesus believed in the reality of floors one and two.
But for him, the realm of the Spirit, the realm
of the Kingdom, was primary. It is not of this
world. And to do work in the third floor
(spiritual work) leads to changes on the other
two floors.

Thus for Jesus, physical healing is best approached
through a spiritual (third floor) angle of attack.
Not through surgery and pills.

For Jesus, a healthy spirit leads to a healthy soul/mind/
heart, which leads to a healthy body.

Pentecostals totally line up with Jesus, not Aristotle
or Plato, on this one. And they are not willing to give
ground.

And any objective observer would see that they have a
point.

Over and over, I have seen people make more physical
healing progress in a twenty-five-minute prayer meeting
than in months of prescription (physical/chemical)
treatment.

In a Pentecostal healing meeting, people lay hands on
others and "go all third floor" on them. They go right
after the spiritual brokenness that may be the root cause
of the disease.

One only has to think of our grossly overweight society, and the massive trillions spent on resulting medical care trying to cure the symptoms caused by obesity, when there is deep inner pain trying to get covered by overeating.

Why not go right to the cause?

Some healthcare problems are caused by terrible misfortune (birth defects, ghastly accidents, ravaging plagues, etc.). But you and I both know that most healthcare problems are brought on by our own self-destructive behavior. And you can make a case that this is because we are, at some level, out of balance spiritually.

Pentecostal prayer meetings attempt to restore the spiritual balance of those for whom they are praying. The resulting physical transformation is often dramatic.

Much of our disease is exacerbated by long-term, chronic stress. Establishing God's peace at our core takes away the food supply that feeds much of our disease.

Inner peace brings amazing health benefits. Pentecostals call this "divine health."

They also have a huge belief in the power of words. More zealous Pentecostals forbid the use of negative self-statements. We will cover more of this in the chapter on the Word/Faith movement.

But this has a lot to do with healing, so we will introduce the idea here.

Those being prayed for are encouraged to speak forth positive things about themselves. Moderates would say things like, "Thank you Jesus for the healing you are doing in my body." Radicals would say, "By Your stripes, Jesus, I am healed, Hallelujah."

Words like "terminal" and "incurable" are taboo.

The Lord's Prayer is also used, frequently, in healing prayer.

There is a potent little phrase that Jesus taught us: "On earth as it is in heaven."

It is common to hear prayers like this:

> *Lord, in heaven there is no cancer, and you command us to pray "on earth as it is in heaven," so we pray heaven into our sister right now—and cancer will have to go, in Jesus' name! Amen.*

Faith doesn't bargain with illness, it expels it.

Uncompromising faith has undoubtedly kept "exceptional patients" alive for decades past their "predicted death date." Many live a normal life span with exceptional faith.

Many of us, perhaps you, too, have observed that when people want to stay alive, they often find a way.

Deep inside Pentecostalism, there is a "depth conviction" that God wants us to be well.

In this way, the Bible is read with John 10:10 at the pivot point. The thief comes to steal, kill, and destroy, but Jesus comes that we might have life— to the fullest.

When it comes to healing, Pentecostalism is deeply dualistic (good and evil) and, thus, sometimes a bit anti-Calvinistic (all is from God).

> Note: There are exceptions to this, such as the Charismatic Calvinist faith family *Sovereign Grace*, but that's the topic of another book.

Bad things don't come from God, in their minds.

God is good, all the time.

When disease hits, God is on our side fighting it with us.

Pentecostals are much like Lutherans in this way. One only need read the words to Martin Luther's classical hymns to taste the deep dualism in his worldview.

> *Though hordes of devils fill this land, all threatening to devour us/A champion comes to fight, with weapons of the Spirit/Lord Zebaoth his name/He holds the field victorious.*

> *Martin Luther: A Mighty Fortress*
> *16th Century Hymn*

Calvinism just doesn't work for most Pentecostal Christians (although there are exceptions). How could God cause or "allow" disease? Calvinism might suggest that God somehow sends disease, even if we don't understand it.

Or how could God "allow" suffering and illness? That would be like a babysitter saying to parents, "I'm sorry that your kids didn't make it through the evening unhurt; I didn't actually cause their injuries—I just allowed the criminals into the house."

Calvinism is a monistic worldview. It doesn't work in a Pentecostal prayer meeting where God is on our side fighting the darkness.

There is a natural theological alliance between Pentecostals, Lutherans, and African-American

Christians. There is a profound theologically genetic "dualism" in all of them.

Go to the office of many Pentecostal pastors, and you will see copies of Lenski's biblical commentaries in the shelves. Lenski is also the dean of Lutheran Bible commentators.

It is also hard for African-American theologians to teach that, somehow, slavery was God's will. The Pharaoh was opposing both us and God.

Pentecostalism is incurably dualistic, and disease will always be an enemy of God.

And God comes alongside us to fight it.

Chapter Seven
DELIVERANCE

Jesus went about casting out demons.

There is no denying that this was one of his major activities.

And it seemed like Jesus thought of it as totally normal.

He clearly taught his disciples to go out and do the same.

But many of today's Christians see demons as a bit anachronistic.

It's a bit odd, at the very least, that contemporary followers of Jesus would think that they have a better understanding of demons than Jesus did.

I was once told by a "modern" pastor, when I was a child, that Jesus "just didn't understand modern psychiatry, and that these people were just mentally ill."

How could the savior of the world have less of a grip on human nature than I have?

But for most of us, the casting out of demons was not a part of our normal Sunday morning liturgy. We didn't practice it as children at Vacation Bible School.

The truth is, many of us are oppressed by demons.

You may say: "Christians can't be oppressed by demons, because they have Jesus." The devil harassed Jesus (in the wilderness) and the main target of demons is the Christian individual.

In fact, the spiritual realm is full of all kinds of things we can't understand.

I have seen "mentally ill" people make more progress in one deliverance session than in years of counseling and medications.

Often, you cannot recognize them the next day. Their faces don't look the same.

There has been a great deal written, in Pentecostal circles, on deliverance. They prefer the word "deliverance" to exorcism.

In practice, much of it is simply not all that dramatic, and certainly not "Hollywood."

No silver crosses, clerical collars, or Elizabethan English commands shouted at demons.

Most people with demons have great pain in their backgrounds. Demons make a deal with them:

> *I will protect you from pain if you let me live near your pain.*

"Strongholds" are built, by the demons, and/or the "host," around this pain.

Bondage is the result. And a lack of ability to love and be loved follows.

The classic Pentecostal book on this is called *The Bondage Breaker* by Neil Anderson.

Deliverance is often a simple session of forgiveness. The "host" is asked to talk about who hurt/abused him or her.

Then he/she is invited, out loud, to speak forgiveness for the abuser/offender. He or she also forgives, out loud, himself or herself for any part played in the hurt.

The hurt is laid at the feet of Jesus, and the newly freed person is invited to walk away free of bondage.

Demons tend to flee when "forgiveness work" takes place and strongholds and bondages are broken.

Demons love garbage. When the garbage is "taken out," they have nothing to "feed on."

Forgiveness is the spiritual equivalent of pulling the thorn out of the lion's paw.

Please understand that forgiving an abuser does not mean trusting that person.

It means, simply, letting the past go. It does not mean submitting to future abuse.

Deliverance is often, simply, the assistance given in helping people shift their emotional base from past hurts into the present.

Grace can only be found in the present.

Unforgiveness has been called "drinking poison and hoping your enemy dies."

Deliverance can be defined as a massive shifting of one's heart into the present.

That is where God lives.

Demons can oppress people who live, trapped, in their past stories. In the present, there is freedom. Deliverance is often just bringing people into the present and into the sunlight.

Chapter Eight
THE WORD-FAITH MOVEMENT

They are all over the television. Word-faith preachers:

"Core" Word-faith teachers
The Kenneths (Copeland, Hagin the Younger, Hagin
the Elder)
Creflo Dollar
Paula White
Jesse Duplantis

"Soft" Word-faith teachers
Joyce Meyer
T.D. Jakes
Joel Osteen
Mac Hammond

Much Word-faith teaching was formulated by E.W.
Kenyon in the first part of the twentieth century.

Word-faith churches are also called "Word" churches or
"Faith" churches. I am not here to endorse their teaching,

but to help you understand this highly nuanced form of Pentecostalism.

They are often maligned as "name it and claim it" or "prosperity" preachers.

Certainly, there are such preachers who cross the line into silliness.

But a great many Word-faith preachers are, actually, more in line with New Testament mentality than many historical church preachers.

The movement grew out of an insight:

> *Faith makes a huge difference in the outcome of life. Having faith and speaking faith can alter almost everything. People in the Bible prayed without being tentative and without asterisks.*

It is, in most cases, when free of its excesses, a theology of courage.

It also tends to take root in more underprivileged areas of the world—places where poverty is a systemic curse that needs to be broken.

It is the opposite of liberal Marxist-based teaching that places the blame, simplistically, at the feet of the rich, who are all "oppressors." Some of that is true, but it is not the whole picture. A lot of people are poor because they have a poverty mentality; for some it is a generations-long curse (e.g., third-generation welfare parents).

Word-faith teaching sets out to break that curse.

Word-faith teaching is maligned by conservative fundamentalist Christians on the one side and by liberal mainline Christians on the other.

But there simply is something to what they are saying.

The basic idea is that the Bible is full of promises.

If we align ourselves, heart-soul-mind-spirit, to these promises, then the course of our lives will change.

Word-faith teaching also has rediscovered *the power of words to craft reality*. Words don't just describe things; they call things into being.

Words (vows) create a marriage. God's spoken words, according to the Bible, created the world. Words create a climate around us.

Words are like the hot waffle iron that shapes the batter of reality.

These teachers encourage their students to avoid, like the plague, negative language.

Negative language, or so the line of thought goes, creates a negative environment, which produces negative results.

The whole idea is to get people to put their heart in the promise and not in the problem.

Much Word-faith teaching overlaps with New Thought (e.g., the *Nautilus* journal) ideas popular in the early twentieth century among secular motivational speakers. The former is more potent than the latter, however, because it:

1) Creates vibrant long-term community (Christian congregations)
2) Uses the Bible as a power tool
3) Has a more developed and sophisticated theological basis (orthodox Christianity)

New Thought doctrine formed the seed-bed for much of what was to come after it, from Peale-Schuller "positive mental attitude culture" to garden-variety New Age empowerment stuff taught at business seminars.

Word-faith Christianity also has some roots in New Thought.

Word-faith teaching has a powerful synergistic relationship with Pentecostalism. For whatever reason,

Word-faith teaching can't gain much traction in Fundamentalist circles, Roman Catholic churches, or mainline Protestant congregations.

Both Word-faith teaching and Pentecostalism share a deep passion for personal empowerment. Most Word-faith churches are Pentecostal, but the reverse is not true (i.e., there are many Pentecostal churches that are not Word-faith). Thus Word-faith teaching can be called a (very disproportionately public and prominent) subset of Pentecostalism.

It also lends itself to producing larger-than-life national-profile teachers and flashy congregations. It works well on television. Well over half of the preachers on current Christian TV shows have serious Word-faith tendencies, although the movement is only a small minority in the American Christian spectrum.

So why is this movement so viciously attacked by the mainline and conservative congregations?

I have an hypothesis.

Western Christianity has *deep blue monastic ink* dyed in its wool. The monasteries kept Christianity alive through the dark ages.

All of that is good.

The dark side of it is that Christianity was so identified with a monastic interpretation that Jesus ended up a wispy St. Francis of Assisi and Christian leaders all ended up taking vows of poverty, chastity, and obedience.

It became an assumption, over the centuries, that to take your faith seriously, you should become a "religious" person, join an order, and give up on the marketplace and family.

Christianity became a religion of escape rather than a lifestyle of incarnation and investment in creation. A self-loathing humbleness became the temperamental ideal: "...that saved a wretch like me..."

Poverty, very simply, became the spiritual goal.

Mainline liberals, to this day, shame the wealthy and imply that they are the cause of most of the world's problems.

Word-faith teaching, on the other hand, revels in abundance. The thinking goes that the best way to help the poor is not to give alms, but rather to help people not to be "one of the poor" in the first place. In their thinking, poverty is a curse, and people need to be taught out of that curse.

To imply that the poor are victims robs them, according to Word-faith thinking, of their empowerment. It reinforces their poverty. It is, in this way, less patronizing than almsgiving or Marxism, which makes the poor believe that it is someone else's fault that they are poor. Victim mentality is not empowerment mentality.

The poor are taught, in Word-faith churches, to stop thinking poor, to stop talking poor, and to stop being poor. Ironically, it is a form of liberation theology— liberation from the inside out.

At its core, Word-faith doctrine insists that God wants us to live in healthy abundance.

It's pretty hard to argue with that, if you sit down and think about it for a while.

If God wants you well and you're not well, then it's not God's fault; or so goes the thinking of the movement.

Healing is another huge Word-faith/Pentecostal overlap zone.

Both movements have strident healing cultures. Word-faith healing focuses on a couple of Bible phrases:

1) By his stripes you are healed.
2) Your faith has made you well.

Healing candidates are encouraged to see themselves as healed, no matter what the "results" look like; to walk by faith and not by sight, until the physical comes around and aligns with the spiritual.

They are also led to believe that their faith, or lack thereof, has a lot to do with their healing.

The argument goes:

1) If you can receive salvation by faith…
2) And have assurance that you have received it…
3) Then you can receive healing by faith in the same way, and with the same confidence.

The problem with this thinking, although there is much about it that works, is that weaker folks will blame themselves if they don't get results. This can lead to a downward spiral of despair.

It's bad enough to be sick without believing that it's your own fault!

There is this core tension in Word-faith churches around healing. But you can't argue with their results. Most Christians in the developing world can name a person or two who has been raised from the dead. They can bring you to where they live and introduce you to them.

Why should this surprise us, if Jesus commanded his disciples to heal the sick and raise the dead?

I would rather err on the side of too much faith (if that is even possible), than err on the side of tentativeness.

One only has to recall the woman in the New Testament with the issue of blood who said to herself: "If I touch the hem of his garment, I will be healed."

And she was.

I want to "get me some of that."

In a nutshell, Word-faith teaching can be reduced to:

1) Identify your need.
2) Find a promise in the Bible that corresponds to your need.
3) Speak that promise forth and believe it.
4) Visualize it as completed regardless of the apparent results.
5) Repeat 1–4 as necessary until the need is met.

It has a dark side, but it can also be a corrective to anemic, escapist Christianity.

Word-faith blood runs very, very red.

Chapter Nine
PRAYER IN THE SPIRIT-FILLED LIFE

In many historical churches, prayer is written, collected, learned, and repeated. Some of these prayers are sublimely crafted and angelic in balance.

In many conservative Evangelical churches, personal prayer time, journaling, and quiet time with God is encouraged. Prayer concerns and lists are compiled.

In Pentecostalism, on the other hand, prayer is an eruption of the Spirit. It is deeply supernatural, non-cognitive, and unpredictable. It is certainly a two-way conversation.

The cool thing about Pentecostal prayer is that it is never, ever boring.

Please review what was said (see above) about the three-story house.

1) The Flesh/Body
2) The Mind/Heart/Emotions/Soul
3) The Spirit

For conservative Evangelicals, much of prayer is a second-story exercise. We gather our thoughts and think them, with discipline, at God. Our expectations of a direct answer are minimal. We keep lists and outlines to keep our thinking from wandering—to keep it on track.

This is how I learned to pray. And it was such hard work. I could never seem to sustain it. Sometimes it felt like an imaginary conversation with an imaginary, silent partner.

After hanging out with Pentecostals, my prayer life took off. I left the second floor, pulled down the attic stairs with a rope, and climbed up into the dusty third floor. I went around and opened windows, and the light and fresh air streamed in.

I learned to be with God; my spirit would commune with his Spirit. He always has more talk than I have listen. And I don't have to tell a story about it or interpret it while it's happening. There would be no way to write a "verbatim" on it, because it's not a writable conversation. It's pre-linguistic.

Paul said he would pray in the Spirit, and pray with his mind also. For him, prayer was primarily a third-floor activity, although he also spent time, apparently, on the second floor too.

Pentecostal prayer can happen one-on-one with God, but it is often driven by the prayer meeting. People receive words; speak and interpret tongues; get prophecies from God directly. They pour their spirits out to God in sounds they don't understand, at least in a cognitive way.

Prayer has been defined, in Pentecostal terms, as an unusually stubborn attempt to abide in the presence of God.

It is third-floor time spent with the windows open.

Anything, yes anything, can happen.

Chapter Ten
CHARISMATIC WORSHIP

Charismatic/Pentecostal worship is deeply African.

This may come as a surprise.

Africa has taken over the global music scene. The African slaves in the Western hemisphere brought their tones, rhythms, and spiritual potency to the melodic and terminal complexity of Western music.

The result has been a revolution.

Virtually nothing musical on the radio in America is free of African influence.

African-American Christianity has also moved in and taken over American church life.

Anglo-Whites are now preaching in the casual linguistic register (as opposed to the formal register). And they are moving around while they talk.

Most American churches now follow, more closely, the prayer and song meeting order of American slaves than they do the mass of Christendom in Europe.

We call it "contemporary worship," when truly speaking, it is simply African.

African-American worship was tailor-made for Pentecostalism.

Go to any Charismatic-Pentecostal worship service, and it will look (even if it is all Anglo-Whites) much more like the worship and teaching style of American slaves than anything else.

The most prominent features are:

1) The pastor preaching in the casual (linguistic) register.
2) Music with a driving rhythm. Drums and bass.
3) Clapping on the second and fourth beats.
4) Hands in the air during singing.
5) Long worship music sets uninterrupted by words/announcements/liturgy
6) High volume sound.
7) Oral/visual culture (screens, "improv" sermons), rather than written culture (hymnbooks, longhand written sermons, etc.)

All of American Christendom has been affected by Africa. But Charismatic/Pentecostal worship has the inside track on this adoption.

But that's just the cultural flavoring and style. The point of Charismatic/Pentecostal worship is to yield to an encounter with the Lord during the music.

Another thing you should know: Pentecostals don't call the whole Sunday morning gathering "worship." That label only applies to the music/singing time. When they say, "It happened today during the worship time," they mean "during the music."

Back to the encounter...

The music leader (often called the "worship pastor") is one of the key leaders in a Pentecostal Church. He or she leads the worship team, which is usually set up like a rock band, instrumentally. One of the most important times on Sunday morning is the "sound check" when all the levels are set before worship begins.

Words are usually (at least in North America) projected on a screen; this allows for freedom of movement for one's hands (clapping, raising).

Although many Pentecostal churches have a gospel choir that "backs up" the worship team, the traditional "anthem choir" is usually totally replaced by the praise band (worship team).

The purpose the worship team has is to create an environment, using music, that makes it both safe and likely for people to encounter God. The lyrics are often deeply personal and relational. The team will model clapping and the raising of hands at certain times.

If you want to watch Pentecostal worship at its spiritual and technical best, I'd invite you to get a recent live worship DVD from Hillsongs Church in Sydney, Australia (*This is Our God*, 2008).

Pentecostal worship has been sneaking into established historical churches, for a generation now, by the "Trojan Horse" known as an "alternative" or "contemporary" service.

This has set up "worship wars" in countless congregations. In a way, you can see it as Euro-centric vs. Afro-centric worship. But it is much more than that. Make no mistake about it, a contemporary service is a missionary beachhead of intentional Pentecostalism in your congregation.

It makes sense for you to try to understand what is behind it!

✳ ✳ ✳

Chapter Eleven
LIFE IN THE SPIRIT

The Pentecostal lifestyle is, at many levels, non- or even anti-religious.

It is not historically oriented. It is not theologically oriented. It is not rules based.

Holiness and lifestyle are taken seriously—very seriously. But they can only be achieved with God's presence and power.

The keen moral insight of Pentecostals is that Jesus was not sinless because he met all the expectations of those around him; he was not a compliance-athlete. He was sinless because he walked with the Father and ignored all of those external expectations coming at him from every direction.

Thus holiness flows out of a vitalized relationship with God. If we are close to God, we cannot sin. The closer we draw to God and abide there, the less we are able to sin at all.

Holiness is not a fruit of the effort. It is a fruit of the Spirit.

The more Spirit, the more holiness.

Efforts to become holy will just get us into trouble and make us unattractive. The result is highly religious hypocrites. Yuck.

According to Paul, so well described in Galatians, we have three choices around which to center our behavior:

1) The flesh.
2) The law.
3) The Spirit.

The right answer, for Pentecostals, would be "door number three."

We get taught the law as we grow up. These expectations start to choke us as we get older. As we escape these collective expectations, our two remaining choices are the flesh and the Spirit.

The parable of the Prodigal Son describes it so well. The closer the son is to the father, the better things go. The farther away he is, the more his behavior unravels.

Holiness is not a matter of discipline.

It is not a matter of effort.

It is a matter of proximity.

Christian lifestyle can only flow out of a vitalized and living relationship with God. No relationship, no holiness—no matter how hard you work at following the rules!

Efforts in rule-following just lead to religiosity and a Pharisee (legalistic) spirit. The pride that comes with this is a powerful people-repellant.

The goal of the Pentecostal life is to learn to listen to one voice in all moral and ethical decisions—the voice of the living God.

For Pentecostals, God is not a god of the hidden face; he is the God of the shining face.

"May his countenance (i.e., face) shine upon you."

This sounds the same as conservative Evangelicalism, but it's not. Many Pentecostals/Charismatics are conservative Evangelicals, and vice versa. But they have different driving motivations.

Conservative Evangelicalism is *contract oriented*. God makes a proposition (the Gospel), and we say yes. We get saved.

This is not what Pentecostals believe or practice. For them, the conservative Evangelical view of a saving contract with God is like a marriage that may or may not have been consummated.

Pentecostalism is all about consummating the marriage with God. There is a (spiritually) erotic nature to it.

Pentecostals live out of an unpredictable relationship with God, not a static, unchanging contract.

The present is everything.

The past is not all that interesting. The Bible is more of a book that helps us encounter God in the present and less of a story that defines us.

Pentecostalism is all about living in the radical present, and building your life around that reality.

Chapter Twelve
LIGHT YOUR CHURCH ON FIRE
WITHOUT BURNING IT DOWN

Well, here we are at the end of our little tour.

Understanding is the first step in any helpful action.

Some practical key pointers for your church:

1) Assume that there are Pentecostals/Charismatics
   in your fellowship. There are a lot more of them
   than you think, and the likelihood of your
   membership being free of them is unlikely.
   Many of them are drawn to traditional, historical
   congregations.
2) Don't lump them in with all conservative
   Evangelicals, many of whom are not Pentecostal/
   Charismatic. Or with TV preachers. Or assume
   they all speak with a Southern accent and vote
   Republican. Stereotypes are not helpful.

3) Use the phrase, "Help me understand…" as often as you can when talking with them. Show genuine interest.

4) Ask them about their encounters with God, not just about their theology and conceptual beliefs. They tend to be way more interested in the former than in the latter.

5) If you are in leadership in your church, do not think of them or speak of them as if they are a threat. They get very defensive around such language. They usually consider themselves harmless in your congregation.

6) Start a prayer ministry around them. They have true gifts in this ministry.

7) Enjoy their generosity. They tend to tithe.

8) They love touch. Put your hand on their shoulder when you make a point. Pat their back when they leave. Hug them when you greet them. They often close a conversation (on the phone or otherwise) with, "Love ya." It can be unnerving if you are physically distant, but it's the way they are, and they don't think of it as sexual.

9) When they talk about needing prayer, they don't want you to write it down and put it on your list. They want you to put your hand on their shoulder and pray now.

10) Ask their opinions on how to improve worship in your church. Don't get defensive.

11) Stop putting down their national leaders or making fun of caricatures of Pentecostals. Many Christians do this without intending.

12) Have them set up stations to pray over people who want prayer after they have received communion (altar rails are great for this).

13) They love serving communion. Invite them.

14) Give them lists of "lost people" to pray over.

15) Invite them to pray over your leaders before every church service. In person.

16) Go with them to Charismatic/Pentecostal gatherings if they invite you. Keep an open mind.

17) Start an Alpha Course (www.Alpha.org) and have them help lead it.

You can run into trouble with Pentecostal/Charismatic Christians in the following ways:

1) Prophecy can be problematic. I'm not talking about predictions of the future, but the gift some people operate in when they speak for God in the present. The ego often gets tied up in the prophecy. Pastoring the prophetic gifts can get dicey. But it's worth it. We are in the presence of a God who speaks.

2) They often talk a lot about "covering," i.e., how your congregation should leave your faith family or denomination because of the denominational leadership being "in rebellion." They see denominational leaders as an authority and "covering" for your ministry. The reasoning goes that if the covering is corrupt, you have to get out from under it, or the "hand of blessing" will

be removed. *Most of this is total hooey.* When Paul went to the Jerusalem church, he commented about those "who seemed to be in authority" but that it didn't matter to him or to God. There is no such thing as a "covering." Christians aren't really in authority over each other; we are to be servants and not "lord it over" anyone. We are brothers and sisters, not parents, in the Lord, with each other. Denominational leadership has been fraught with problems forever, and is not a good enough reason to get all "defection" oriented and schismatic.

3) Pentecostals and Charismatics are often insensitive toward seekers and visitors. They might go into a "happy dance" during worship in a way that attracts way too much attention to themselves and freaks out the visitors. They need to be coached through this without dampening their spirits. Of course, this depends on your cultural setting and how inhibited or uninhibited it may be.

4) They can get so obsessed with healing that it's all they do. Once a person is healed (in the present) they may go after all kinds of past hurts, sometimes even re-creating "womb" healing experiences that are not all that different from New Age past-incarnation cleansings. Healings can become a Zeno's paradox of infinite self-absorption, which keeps the focus off of loving others, reaching the lost, and moving the Kingdom forward.

5) Sometimes, schizophrenia and other mental illness, especially when the person diagnosed with these diseases uses a lot of Bible sound bites, can sound like Pentecostalism, but there's nothing spiritual going on. Sometimes medical/psychiatric treatment is necessary in these cases.

There will be more books in this series, but this is a good start. Buy a copy for your friends and help make understanding the first step toward love and fellowship among all followers of Jesus.

Pentecostalism is a wonderful move of God, don't miss it!

Quench not the Spirit!
—The Apostle Paul, first century A.D.

Chapter Thirteen
VOCABULARY AND PHRASE GUIDE

Anointing: One of the most common Pentecostal terms. An effortless sense of God's power when leading worship, teaching, preaching, or praying over people. A anointed leader is someone who operates in God's power, and not his or her own strength.

Alpha Course: The primary evangelistic tool used by many Charismatic Christians (and many others). Started thriving in London in the 1990s.

Baptism in the Holy Spirit: The central experience of yielding to God. Often roughly synonymous with Spirit filling.

Bridge: Part of a contemporary praise song not found in traditional hymns. Different from the verses or a chorus. A place in the song with a different melody or message used as contrast to the rest of the song.

Carpet Time: Synonymous with being "slain in the Spirit" or "resting in the Spirit." Collapsing to the ground and spending time in the presence of the Lord.

Cessationism: A form of theology, associated with dispensationalism, that teaches that healing and tongues are not for today. There are more and less strict camps within this thinking. This theology is the arch-enemy of Pentecostalism.

Charismatic: A movement, denomination, or person that identifies with Pentecostalism but generally fits within established faith families. Usually, but not always, a little more understated than Pentecostalism. Taken from the Greek word "charism," which means both "grace" and "gift."

Deliverance: The preferred Pentecostal term for "exorcism" or the casting out of demons.

Fire Baptism: The Bible contrasts water baptism with fire (Spirit) baptism. What looked like flames appeared above the heads of the apostles at Pentecost.

Generational Curse/Blessings: Patterns handed down from previous generation, e.g., the reality that children of alcoholics and abusers have a higher likelihood of suffering from the same disorders and passing them to their children.

Glossolalia: Speaking, singing, or praying in tongues. Expressing oneself vocally without the benefit of vocabulary or grammar.

Holy Ghost: Term in the King James Bible for "Holy Spirit." Used less and less over time.

Ministry Time: A time for people to get prayer from (usually trained) prayer ministers.

Oneness Pentecostal: Pentecostals who de-emphasize the Trinity and baptize in the name of Jesus, not in the name of the Father, Son, and Holy Spirit.

Pentecostal: A movement, denomination, or person that identifies with and emphasizes healings, speaking in tongues, and Spirit filling as central parts of their faith expression. Taken from the word "Pentecost," the festival celebrating the events of Acts chapter 2 in the New Testament.

Power Evangelism: Evangelizing, not just by teaching or deeds of love and mercy, but by demonstrating God's power through signs, wonders, and healings.

Praise and Worship: The prevailing Pentecostal/ Charismatic worship style; non-Pentecostals call it "contemporary worship."

Praise Set: An extended session, often without a break, of singing at least a few songs in succession.

Prophecy: Speaking directly for God. Not necessarily, as in popular speech, predicting the future.

Prophetic Worship: Worship that is less planned and more reliant on God directing the worship pastor from moment to moment.

Resting in the Spirit: Synonymous with being "slain in the Spirit" or "carpet time." Collapsing to the ground and spending time in the presence of the Lord.

Rhema: What God is saying now. Pentecostals contrast this with "logos," or the word spoken by God at all times to all people. Other Christians don't make this distinction as clearly.

Singing in the Spirit: Alone or in a group: Singing spontaneously, usually without the benefit of vocabulary or grammar. Synonymous with "singing in tongues."

Slain in the Spirit: Synonymous with doing "carpet time" or "resting in the Spirit." Collapsing to the ground and spending time in the presence of the Lord.

Shekinah (Glory): The cloud of God's presence.

Spirit Filling: The central experience of yielding to God. Often roughly synonymous with "baptism in the Holy Spirit."

Spiritual Warfare: Background is Ephesians 6:10ff and other passages. Anything having to do with fighting the devil and/or demons.

Stronghold: A part of your life where the Devil has a foothold.

Third Wave: A part, like "Pentecostal" and "Charismatic" of the same basic "batch" of Christians. A later development in the movement, focused around Vineyard Churches and the Toronto Blessing (you can look up both of these on Wikipedia).

Toronto Blessing: A long-running revival at the Toronto Airport Christian Fellowship. Edgy and unpredictable, one of the hallmarks has been "holy laughter."

Word: When someone says "I (may) have a Word," they mean a message directly from God.

Word of Knowledge: A direct piece of information from God to an individual. Something that he or she could not have learned in the natural. Related to a "word of wisdom." Words of knowledge are often used to prompt prayers for healing.

Word of Wisdom: A less specific Word of Knowledge. Usually referring to a general truth which God gives supernaturally to a person.

Word-faith (or simply "Faith," or "Word"): A subset of Pentecostalism that focuses on the promises of God, especially for healing and prosperity.

Worship Team: Synonymous with Praise Band. A contemporary worship group with electronic rock instrumentation.

Worship Time: The musical portion of a church service or meeting.

BIBLIOGRAPHY AND SUGGESTED READING

I would like to thank all the following authors for giving me a vocabulary to express what I felt God was doing in my life.

Fire from Heaven
Harvey Cox
Da Capo/Perseus Books, Cambridge, MA, 1995

The Bondage Breaker
Neil T. Anderson
Harvest House, Eugene, OR, 1990, 1993, 2000

Questions of Life
Nicky Gumbel
David C. Cook, Colorado Springs, CO, 1993, 1996

Sober Intoxication of the Spirit: Filled with the Fullness of God
Raniero Cantalamessa
Servant Books, Cincinnati, OH, 2005

The Century of the Holy Spirit: 100 Years of Pentecostal and Charismatic Revival

Vinson Synan
Thomas Nelson, Nashville, TN, 2001

David Housholder was born in Idaho, USA, and raised in
a traditional Lutheran church environment.

He came into direct contact with Pentecostal Christianity
while planting a church in rural Washington State, and
has been traveling the world and teaching on both sides
of the Pentecostal/mainstream "spiritual fence" ever
since.

He earned his Master of Divinity at Chicago's Lutheran
School of Theology and was a Fulbright scholar in
New Testament at the University of Bonn, Germany.

A pastor of the Evangelical Lutheran Church in
America and the Alliance of Renewal Churches, he is an
international conference speaker and author of the Galatians
portion of *Augsburg/Fortress Book of Faith* series (2009).

Today he lives in Huntington Beach, California, where he
works as a church planter at Robinwood Church and surfs
the waves with his friends on most days. David and his
wife, Wendy, have one son, Lars.

3964134

Made in the USA